GIRAFFES
AND THEIR BABIES

MARIANNE JOHNSTON

The Rosen Publishing Group's
PowerKids Press™
New York

Special thanks to Diane Shapiro of the Bronx Zoo for making this project possible.

Published in 1999 by The Rosen Publishing Group, Inc.
29 East 21st Street, New York, NY 10010

First Edition

Book Design: Resa Listort

Photo Credits: All photos © Wildlife Conservation Society.

Johnston, Marianne.
    Giraffes and Their Babies / by Marianne Johnston.
        p.   cm. — (A zoo life book)
    Includes index.
    Summary: Describes the characteristics of giraffes and how mother giraffes living in zoos are taught to care for their babies.
    ISBN 0-8239-5316-5
    1. Giraffe—Juvenile literature. 2. Giraffe—Infancy—Juvenile literature. 3. Zoo animals—Juvenile literature. [1. Giraffe. 2. Animals—Infancy. 3. Zoo animals.] I. Title. II. Series: Johnston, Marianne. Zoo life book.
    QL737.U56C725 1998
    599.638—DC21   98-23985
                                                                              CIP
                                                                              AC

Manufactured in the United States of America

CONTENTS

THE GIRAFFE

Giraffes are the tallest land animals in the world. Most giraffes grow to be sixteen to eighteen feet tall. The tallest giraffe known to man was nineteen feet tall. A giraffe's long neck has the same number of bones as a human's neck does. But a giraffe's neck grows to be longer than the height of an adult human!

Giraffes once lived all over Africa and in parts of Asia and Europe. Today giraffes live on the grasslands of southern and eastern Africa, as well as in small parts of central Africa. Giraffes can also be found in zoos all around the world.

ORDER:
ARTIODACTYLE
FAMILY:
GIRAFFIDAE
GENUS & SPECIES:
GIRAFFA CAMELOPARDALIS

◀ Male giraffes are called bulls. Females are called cows.

WHAT ARE GIRAFFES LIKE?

Giraffes are **browsers** (BROW-zurz). They eat twigs and leaves from the highest branches of trees. The **acacia** (ah-KAY-shuh) tree is a favorite of giraffes. Acacias grow on the grasslands in Africa, where many giraffes live.

There is only one **species** (SPEE-sheez) of giraffe. Within that species, there are nine different types of giraffes. You can tell them apart by the different patterns and colors of their coats. The Masai giraffe has dark brown, jagged spots on its coat. The coat of the **reticulated** (reh-TIK-yoo-lay-ted) giraffe is covered with reddish brown shapes that have smooth edges.

A giraffe's tongue can be eighteen inches long. This helps the giraffe grab onto treetop snacks. ▶

BORN TO BE WILD

After a female giraffe **mates** (MAYTS), she will be **pregnant** (PREG-nunt) for about fifteen months. That's more than a year! When she is ready to give birth to her baby, the giraffe finds a private place, like a section of tall grass.

It takes about an hour for a giraffe to give birth. The mother stands the whole time as she works hard to bring her baby into the world. The calf enters the world by falling down six feet to the ground. After the birth, the mother quickly licks the baby clean. A baby giraffe, or **calf** (KAF), is already six feet tall at birth.

Even though giraffes are social animals, the males and females usually live in different areas.

MOTHER GIRAFFES IN A ZOO

When zookeepers know that a female giraffe is pregnant, they watch for signs that she is ready to give birth. One sign is that her **udder** (UH-der) gets bigger. This means the udder is filling up with milk for the newborn calf to drink.

When a giraffe is going to have her baby, zookeepers move the mother to a private place. This keeps the mother away from the rest of the giraffes. This also keeps zoo visitors away from the giraffe. A mother giraffe must not be upset when she is giving birth.

Giraffes are among the few animals that are born with horns. ▶

BORN IN A ZOO

Once the mother giraffe has been moved into a stall, zookeepers get ready for the birth. The floor of the stall is covered with a thick layer of soft straw. Like giraffes in the wild, zoo giraffes also give birth while they're standing. Zookeepers put down the straw to make sure the calf has a soft landing.

Once the birth begins, zookeepers watch from a hidden place to make sure everything is okay. When the baby is finally born, the mother licks her calf clean, just like mother giraffes do in the wild.

◀ A giraffe gives birth to just one baby at a time.

THE FIRST FEW WEEKS

Zookeepers watch the new mother giraffe closely to see that she is caring for her calf. They also find out if the calf has begun to **nurse** (NURS), or drink milk from its mother. If zookeepers see these things happening, they know that the birth has gone well.

During the first couple of weeks of a young giraffe's life, zookeepers **isolate** (EYE-suh-layt) the mother and calf. They are kept away from the rest of the **herd** (HURD) and from visitors to the zoo. When the baby giraffe is able to move around and follow its mother without any problems, zookeepers let the mother and baby return to the herd.

Like giraffe moms in the wild, zoo giraffes stay alone with the calf at first. ▶

THE FIRST YEAR

In the wild, a mother giraffe takes her newborn calf to a hiding place, such as tall grass, for the first month of the baby's life. The calf is not yet strong enough to keep up with the herd or run away from **predators** (PREH-duh-terz), such as lions. A mother giraffe returns a few times a day to feed the calf. At night, the mother watches over her sleeping calf. After a month, the calf will be ready to join other mothers and their calves. Together they form a group that stays together for about a year.

◄ In a group of giraffe mothers and calves, the mothers take turns baby-sitting the calves during the day.

GROWING UP IN A ZOO

In a zoo, mother giraffes don't have to worry about protecting their calves from predators. But they are still very protective of their calves. A mother giraffe carefully watches any new creature or person that goes near her calf. In the zoo, calves run and play just like they do in the wild. They are very curious. Calves spend a lot of time looking and sniffing around their new homes. At four months old, a calf is eating leaves and grass. The calf drinks its mother's milk only when it is thirsty.

By the time a giraffe calf is a year old, it has stopped drinking its mother's milk. ▶

HABITS OF THE GIRAFFE

By the time a giraffe turns two years old, it can take care of itself. But its mother will still nuzzle it. When a giraffe is four years old, it is all grown up.

Giraffes sleep only about a half hour each day. They take several five-minute naps. Giraffes don't often lie down when they go to sleep. It takes a lot of effort for giraffes to stand up on their long legs.

Giraffes live in herds. A giraffe may live with one herd for a while, and then move on to another herd. In the wild, there is always one member of a herd watching out for predators when the other giraffes are eating or sleeping.

◀ A giraffe's hoof is the size of a dinner plate.

THE GIRAFFE'S FUTURE

Giraffes are not an **endangered** (en-DAYN-jurd) species. There are almost 100,000 giraffes living in the wild today. And there are 1,000 more living in zoos. In Africa, there are laws that keep hunters from killing too many giraffes. Sadly, **poachers** (POH-cherz) continue to kill giraffes for their meat, skins, and the hair on their tails.

More and more people are taking over land in Africa. People who want to protect wildlife are working hard to set aside land for parks where giraffes and other animals will be safe.

WEB SITE

You can learn more about giraffes at this Web site: http://planetpets.simplenet.com/plntgraf.htm

GLOSSARY

acacia (ah-KAY-shuh) A tall, wide-branched tree.

browser (BROW-zur) An animal that eats leaves, twigs, and branches from trees and small plants.

calf (KAF) A baby giraffe.

endangered (en-DAYN-jurd) When something is in danger of no longer existing.

herd (HURD) A group of the same kind of animals living together.

isolate (EYE-suh-layt) To place apart and alone.

mate (MAYT) A special joining of a male and female body. Afterward, the female may have a baby grow inside her.

nurse (NURS) When a female gives her baby milk from her body.

poacher (POH-cher) A person who illegally kills animals.

predator (PREH-duh-ter) An animal that kills other animals for food.

pregnant (PREG-nunt) When a female has a baby growing inside her.

reticulated (reh-TIK-yoo-lay-ted) A kind of giraffe that has reddish brown spots divided by thin white lines.

species (SPEE-sheez) A group of animals that are very much alike.

udder (UH-der) The organ that holds milk in animals like giraffes.

23

INDEX